WAWA - TRANSLATED BY HENRY WEI LEUNG

猴王彼彼 - PEI PEI THE MONKEY KING

Wawa (also published as Lo Mei Wa) is a Hong
Kong poet. She received degrees in Philosophy
from the Chinese University of Hong Kong and
Universiteit Leiden, Netherlands. She has been a
singer, a lyricist, an art and design magazine editor,
and a cowherd. Her poems have been featured
in various art exhibits, and in a Radiophrenia
Glasgow broadcast. She has lived in Köln and
Pengchau, and now lives in Honolulu.

Henry Wei Leung is the author of *Paradise Hunger*
(Swan Scythe, 2012) and the recipient of Kundiman,
Soros, and Fulbright fellowships. His poems, essays,
and translations have appeared in such journals as
the *Berkeley Poetry Review*, *Drunken Boat*, and *The
Offing*. He is currently the Managing Editor of
the *Hawai'i Review*.

猴王彼彼

-

W A W A

-

P E I

P E I

T H E

M O N K E Y

K I N G

-

2

PEI PEI THE
MONKEY KING
by Wawa
translated by Henry Wei Leung
Copyright © 2016 | All rights reserved
ISBN-13: 978-0-9891861-9-3

Tinfish Press is a 501(c)3 non-profit, tax-exempt
corporation that supports the publication of
experimental poetry from the Pacific. Tinfish
books are available from Small Press Distribution
in Berkeley, California (spdbooks.org) and from
our website.

TINFISH PRESS
Susan M. Schultz, Editor
47-728 Hui Kelu St. #9
Kāne'ohe, Hi. 96744
press.tinfish@gmail.com

Designed by Jeff Sanner

Support from the John Wythe White & Victoria
Gail-White's Left Wing Right Brain Fund of the
Hawai'i Community Foundation.

www.tinfishpress.com

TRANSLATOR'S INTRODUCTION

We were sitting at a shoreline behind the protest camp in Admiralty when my friend, the writer David William Hill, made a funny observation about Chinese. Suppose, he said, you put three basically literate provincials in a room together, one each from mainland China, Taiwan, and Hong Kong. C and T can converse aloud but can't read each other's writing. T and H can read each other but can't converse. H and C can't communicate at all. Yet all three of them are using "Chinese." The scenario, of course, isn't quite accurate—the fates of these three places overlap and have relatively cosmopolitan literacies—but in its hyperbole, it exposes something about what we assume to be singularly Chinese. When we see, "Translated from the Chinese," it would be prudent to ask: "Which Chinese?" It's much more than a matter of spoken dialects.

Chinese is not a language but an imperial project. As a written form, it dates back to early dynastic times, when a script we now call 1) Classical Chinese was introduced to unify a vast region's panoply of languages. More *scripta franca* than *lingua franca*, it was a literacy for the elites and in no way reflected how people spoke. Then came modernization, the twentieth century, the May Fourth Movement, and Classical's replacement with 2) Baihua, which vernacularized writing by matching it to speech. One of the slogans from that time is telling: "我手寫我口" ("my hand writes my mouth"). The speech of choice, though, was a refined version of the Beijing intellectuals' Mandarin:

in other words, still elite to a degree that what resulted was normative though not necessarily representative. Then came the civil war which ended in 1949, and Baihua divided into two scripts. The Nationalist Party, which left to build its nation in Taiwan, maintained the written form as it was, which we now call 3) Traditional Chinese characters, sometimes called orthodox, full, or complex characters. The Communist Party, which remained to rule mainland China, instituted a radically systematic change now referred to as 4) Simplified Chinese characters. Conversion software would have us believe that the difference between Traditional and Simplified is as negligible as that between the American "gray" and the British "grey." But whole etymologies have been erased in Simplified, and new etymologies have been created, and in the process the lexicon has drifted such that some words are no longer mutually intelligible. At its most mundane, the difference is like that between "trucks" and "lorries." At an extreme, it's like the English "also" and the Middle English "eke."

I've named four Chineses already and haven't even gotten to Hong Kong yet, which existed in an achronicity while all this transpired. The territory of Hong Kong was ceded from dynastic China to the United Kingdom in 1841 after the Opium Wars, and from that point until as late as 1974 (we are now skipping over all of China's modern history and coming in at the end of the Cultural Revolution), Chinese was not an officially recognized language. For our purposes now, we have to consider at least two more Chineses. One is 5) Cantonese, a Chinese spoken dialect which enjoys the unique distinction of having a corresponding written form. This written form is partly an atavism reaching back to older etymologies, partly a *re*-composition of the Chinese character, and more recently includes an admixture of English alphanumerics as well. Its rich history dates back at least to the early 1800s; as a written vernacular it fully reflects the unique speech of Cantonese, the mother tongue for most in Hong Kong.[1] Next, we have to consider what Hongkongers generally refer to as 6) "written Chinese." The ethnologist Chin Wan-kan has argued that colonial Hong Kong's *non*-recognition of Chinese enabled a temporary fossilization—as opposed to the revolutions across the border where linguistic change was systemic. He places the writing in Hong Kong somewhere between "a stricter form of *baihua* or a plainer form of classical Chinese," with a lasting influence: "Official documents and even public announcements in Chinese have been written and read in Hong Kong, until now, mostly in the grammar and vocabulary of plain classical Chinese which bears virtually no affiliation to any spoken dialect."[2] He maintains that, were it not for the economic boom of the 1980s and the cultural export of Cantonese, among other factors, Hong Kong might have

[1] For more, see Donald B. Snow, *Cantonese as Written Language: The Growth of a Written Chinese Vernacular* (Hong Kong: Hong Kong University Press, 2004).

[2] Chin Wan-kan, "From Dialect to Grapholect: Written Cantonese from a Folkloristic Viewpoint," *Hong Kong Journal of Applied Linguistics* 2.2 (1997): 78-9.

persisted as a *Sprachinsel*—a language island—for the preservation of Classical Chinese. (It is worth observing the politics underlying his scholarship, as Chin is a controversial proponent for radical sentiments of Hong Kong nationalism.) Written Chinese in Hong Kong developed and evolved, and unlike the Classical of dynastic times, it belongs to such a broadly literate society that it's what we find written in newspapers, books, and karaoke-screen pop songs. And, significantly, its characters are pronounced aloud in Cantonese rather than Mandarin.

So when I say that *Pei Pei the Monkey King* is written somewhere along the spectrum between Chinese #5 and Chinese #6, I mean that readers in, say, Taiwan, will understand the gist of what they read but will *hear* and experience the poems very differently from readers in Hong Kong. This raises funny questions for translation: we're used to talking about what's lost in the transfer from Chinese to English, but how about what's lost from Chinese to Chinese?

Hong Kong's current policy of *biliteracy* (Chinese, English) and *trilingualism* (Cantonese, Mandarin, English) leaves the umbrella term "Chinese" ambiguous enough to have allowed for Cantonese to be gradually displaced by Mandarin. As my diverging histories demonstrate, the common assumption which conflates Hong Kong's written Chinese with the Chinese of the mainland is politically guided and basically untenable. Alarms have been raised by language concern groups at the increased use of Mandarin as the "Chinese" language of instruction in Hong Kong schools—often encouraged by government subsidies and suggestive of a greater cultural displacement.[3] And as Rey Chow has written: "Known in the People's Republic by its egalitarian-sounding appellation Putonghua (common speech), the hegemony of Mandarin has been made possible through its identification more or less with the written script . . . Mandarin is, properly speaking, also *the white man's Chinese*, the Chinese that receives its international authentication as 'standard Chinese.'"[4] There is a shop-worn discourse of victimization which marginalizes Hong Kong between two colonial powers, one consequence of which is what Mirana May Szeto calls a dysfunctional "petit-grandiose Hong Kongism," or the aggrandizement of such marginality to the point of pride.[5] It is the pride of "hybridity," which essentially reifies colonial structures in which Hong Kong is the best and worst of East and West, but never anything *in and of itself*. How might Hong Kong sound if it were not merely an echo? To hear this would require us to listen more closely to "Chinese," divesting the term of its national and political costuming. Thus Lo Kwai-Cheung: "The pluralism or multiplicity of Chinese identities only presents more choices for

---

[3] Elaine Yau and Vanessa Yung, "Cantonese or Putonghua in Schools? Hongkongers Fear Culture and Identity 'waning,'" *South China Morning Post* (2 Sep 2014).

[4] Rey Chow, "On Chineseness as a Theoretical Problem," *Sinophone Studies: A Critical Reader*, eds. Shumei Shi, Chien-hsin Tsai, and Brian Bernards (New York: Columbia University Press, 2013): 47-8.

[5] Mirana May Szeto, "Identity Politics and Its Discontents: Contesting Cultural Imaginaries in Contemporary Hong Kong," *Interventions* 8.2 (2006): 272.

a general idea of 'Chineseness,' which, instead of providing anything precise, simply conceals the fact that 'Chineseness' is an empty term."[6]

In an essay from earlier this year, published under the name Lo Mei Wa and addressed to an imagined future daughter, Wawa says: "Now I only want to be a Hongkonger and swear in Cantonese. I have to teach you this language before a day comes when I might be arrested for speaking it. . . . We, Hongkongers, are becoming forced-Chinese."[7] Listen carefully again: if Chineseness is an empty signifier, then what Wawa resists here is not a multivalent two-thousand-year history, but its simplification and flattening by the Communist Party on the mainland. That Chineseness can be forced at all is another indicator of the imaginaries being shaped here. The territory of Hong Kong was returned from Britain to China in the 1997 Handover, and currently operates under fifty years of quasi-autonomous rule. But the dynastic China from which Hong Kong had been taken no longer existed in 1997, and Hong Kong developed in its own bubble of history, at times in opposition to mainland China. Some of the more obvious instances of this would be the flight of mainlanders to Hong Kong during the Cultural Revolution, or Operation Yellowbird in which Hong Kong offered safe haven for dissidents at Tiananmen Square. The annual June Fourth Vigil held in Victoria Park after 1989, as well as the recent controversy of its disruption

[6] Lo Kwai-Cheung, *Chinese Face/Off: The Transnational Popular Culture of Hong Kong* (Chicago: University of Illinois, 2005): 6.

[7] Lo Mei Wa, "Letter to a Future Daughter on the Occasion of the "Fishball Revolution," *Guernica Daily* (29 Feb 2016).

earlier this year—by masked men who charged the stage saying that June Fourth is China's affair and not the concern of Hongkongers—speaks to some of the complexity in this opposition. So those who frame the 1997 Handover as a return to a motherland are yanking Hong Kong out of its achronicity and folding it into mainland China's chronology. It is worth distinguishing between the history of a place and the history of the nation which occupies that place; while maps have been redrawn to include Hong Kong within China, "China" itself is a discontinuity of national ruptures precluding any fixed entity to which Hong Kong could "return." And the border has become increasingly sensitive as the "one country, two systems" framework is shown to be ambiguous and contested in practice. Some recent instances of social unrest concerning this sensitive border include the Article 23 Anti-Subversion Bill (2002), the Moral & National Education Scheme (2011), and of course the issue of universal suffrage which led to the Umbrella Revolution/Movement (2014). Ackbar Abbas, who has described Hong Kong's relationship to mainland China as "the strange dialectic between autonomy and dependency," notes the historical oddity of a colonized state which, though politically subordinate, "is in many other crucial respects *not* in a dependent subaltern position but is in fact more advanced—in terms of education, technology, access to international networks, and so forth—than the colonizing state."[8] Writing in the countdown to 1997, he identified the origin of Hong Kong's identity in its *future* specter of

[8] Ackbar Abbas, *Hong Kong: Culture and the Politics of Disappearance* (Minneapolis: University of Minnesota Press, 1997): 5-6.

disappearance. Such a specter looms larger now in the countdown to 2047, at which point Hong Kong will be fully absorbed into China. Recent protests against mainland Chinese interference have helped to refine and codify a certain Hongkongness, which also makes 2047 more absurd. The year is an expiration date: in three decades, Hong Kong as a semi-self-determining entity will simply cease to exist. This specter of expiration—even "extinction" according to some protest signage—might go toward explaining why the city's discourse of protest is so dire.

I got to know Wawa because of the 2014 Umbrella protests, and the discussion of Hong Kong politics has guided much of our relationship since then. I was there on a Fulbright grant intending to study the local literature, and instead ended up spending my days in the Admiralty protest encampment ("Umbrella Plaza," among its many monikers) and my nights in the Mong Kok one ("Pok-Head Square," etc). Though I passed as a local student, I was among those concerned foreigners who—like my friend David who volunteered to haul trash from Admiralty every day—wanted to help and, above all, to understand.[9] I was living a few blocks from Mong Kok in a Kafkaesque "butchered" apartment (劏房) where I often woke to the screams of a neighbor who didn't exist, and where in the later stage of the protests my daily route was controlled by the ID checks of an Orwellian white terror. Wawa, a nervous

---

[9] None of these statements reflects the views or non-views of the U.S. Department of State.

recluse by disposition, was living on a remote, outlying island from which she commuted by ferry every day for work and protest. On September 28, following weeks of rallies and a student strike and teach-in contesting the bogus universal suffrage offered by mainland China to Hong Kong, tear gas was launched at crowds of demonstrators in the street. The deliberative and nonviolent Satyagraha of the protests was characterized by that night's iconic image of protesters defending themselves from the police with only their everyday collapsible umbrellas as shields. That same night, a two-and-a-half-month Occupy campaign commenced and made Hong Kong history. Even the landscape changed. To this day, renegade yellow banners carrying an Umbrella icon and the slogan, "我要真普選" ("I want genuine universal suffrage"), are still occasionally hung from the symbolic mountain peak of Lion Rock—whose "Lion Rock spirit" is Hong Kong's unique version of tenaciously rising above one's birth. More recently, a yellow banner was hung there which read, "我們都是林榮基" ("We are all Lam Wing Kee"), referring to the Hong Kong banned-bookstore manager who just escaped from his abduction by mainland Chinese agents. Lion Rock is a sensitive site whose stage was reset by the Umbrella protests, and now continues to evolve. In a sense, its bluffs are the last soapbox remaining from the Occupy camps.

The poet's foreword to *Pei Pei* locates us on the same mountain "in 2016 after an outbreak of warfare," alluding to the Fishball Riot in Mong Kok on February 8. It was the first riot in fifty years, marked by burning in the streets and warning shots fired by the police. The event might appear like an isolated outburst—ostensibly the issue was only the brutal persecution of unlicensed street hawkers during the Lunar New Year—but the subsequent radicalization of political parties which now dare to speak of Hong Kong independence, the rise to prominence of HK Indigenous (本土民主前線) which had been partly responsible for the riot, and the attention given to one of its young organizers in a by-election campaign for the Legislative Council shortly afterward—all this puts the riot in the same constellation of the political atmosphere I have been describing. Wawa, who had been teargassed with the first crowds of protesters in Admiralty in 2014, draws in her essay a direct connection between Umbrella and Fishball, criticizing the knee-jerk simplicity of those who dismissed the riot. Rather than condemn it for its violence, she wanted to understand the heart of it: "The Umbrella protests were peaceful, rational," she writes, "and ended infernally. It was easy to join the Umbrella comrades then: it was non-violent and intellectual. But reason has been proven madness by our crippled government." To paraphrase the Nietzschean framework, the Umbrella protests were Apollonian: rational, orderly, aimed at a teleological end. The Fishball Riot was Dionysian: irrational, chaotic, with no clear aim or end. The energy of the latter was already latent in the former, which lost by attrition and failed to spur on reform. The continuity between the two might be a balancing of scales. If we understand Hong Kong's thirty remaining years as a kind of mortality, a tragic finitude, then we might understand the riot as an outpouring of the infinite. The riot was not aesthetically digestible the way the Umbrella tent cities were. But it was a demonstration of something governmentality could not circumscribe.

The poems in *Pei Pei* are not political poems in the strict sense. They are not likely to be chanted in a street demonstration, nor are they topical commentaries. However, Hong Kong's political atmosphere so permeates the poems—and Wawa as a person—that their complexity will be lost on a reader unfamiliar with the context. Wawa assures me, for instance, that her sardonic line, "撐起鐵傘" ("Raise the steel umbrella"), was not intended as an allusion to the cheery anthem of the Umbrella protests, "撐起雨傘" ("Raise the [rain] umbrella"). Yet the echo is unmistakable. And the suicides, which are neither subjects nor objects but literally become the landscape of the poems, must also be understood in terms of Hong Kong's specific context. As for other allusions, we would not be wrong to remember the Monkey King from *Journey to the West*, Sun Wukong. But a reader familiar with the classical traditions will find something not quite "Chinese," nor quite "Western," in the fabulistic world constructed here. The childlike tone in many of the poems offers the reader an easy point of entry, but the dark energy conjured by that tone also leads us into something more enigmatic. We might identify influences of Lorca, of Roethke, of Blake; the playful Hong Kong author 西西 (whose pen name literally means "West West") is almost certainly alluded to in the Dong Dong ("East East") Gramma poem; and the first section opens with what is probably the *Zhuangzi*'s mythological bird speaking in the language of the New Testament. But these reverberating threads are everywhere in the poet's words; it would be difficult to box the whole of *Pei Pei* into a single literary tradition or genre. Perhaps it would suffice to say that these are very Hong Kong poems. By this, however, I do not mean the disconnected literature of expatriates, nor the displaced literature of migrant workers sending worlds home, nor the touristic literature produced for export abroad. I mean the very idiom of a very Cantonese city-state is given place and consciousness here, with a sincere tug at the primordial. Those surprised by the bank-and-mall city's protests will be surprised by these poems too, these poems which imitate nothing and defer to no one and are an *ars poetica* of their own.

I'm glad the poems will be presented bilingually here, for I experience much of their vibrancy—as with Hong Kong's—in the deep silence between languages. As Gayatri Spivak has written, "Language is not everything.

It is only a vital clue to where the self loses its boundaries."[10] Spivak here is interested in translation as a theory by which one might read the unreadable self. But divesting one's mother tongue is a condition of exile, and to "write Chinese" in Hong Kong is a thing of many layers. For a Hongkonger, translation might instead be a theory by which to write the self, and as such the poems which follow were already slipping from their boundaries long before any English arrived.

---

[10] Gayatri Chakravorty Spivak, "The Politics of Translation," *Translation Studies Reader*, ed. Lawrence Venuti (United Kingdom: Routledge, 2000): 398.

猴王彼彼

-

WAWA

-

PEI

PEI

THE

MONKEY

KING

-

16

TABLE OF CONTENTS

給香港的孩子、好人、動物和花草樹木

序言

二零一六年，在香港爆發戰爭後，我回到獅子山玩耍。由於多次跟馬騮對望後被追趕，我變得很害怕馬騮。有時在林中吃腸仔包，知道有馬騮從大石後偷望，我都會裝模作樣地慢慢收起麵包，背向而坐，麵包屑留給膽小的彩鳥。

FOREWORD

In Hong Kong in 2016 after an outbreak of warfare, I returned to Lion Rock to play. On account of making eye contact with monkeys and being chased many times, I became afraid of monkeys. Sometimes in the woods, I ate my hot dog *bao* knowing full well that a monkey was stealing a peek from behind some rock. Unflappably, I would palm my *bao* and swivel away, leaving breadcrumbs for timid, colorful birds.

· I

失憶草

大鳥安慰道
牠便是時間
是高空
是大地
於是我便捉緊牠尾巴
從遠方飛到大雨裡
抓著每一片樹葉來看
按著每一只螞蟻來望
風景卻在發呆

我唯有在霧裡靠指尖探路
並一次又一次
被一地打開的行李箱拌倒
好不容易
終於找到一株相熟的小草
他站在山上
在風中搖晃
我激動地向他說
我回來了
他在風中搖晃

小草 我回來了
他在風中搖晃

FORGETTING GRASS

The great bird sayeth consolingly unto me
That he is, well, the Sky, the Time, and
    the Earth
And so I grab hold of his tail
Fly from a faraway place into the downpour
And grab every leaf of tree, gaping
And press down each little ant, poring
Though the landscape spaces out

In the fog I can only count on my fingertip
    to lead the way
Once and again I trip
On this earth of suitcases spilt open
Finally finding against all odds
One blade of grass whom I knew well
He stands on the mount
Shuddering in wind
I burst out saying
I have returned
He shudders in the wind

Little grass, I have returned
He shudders in the wind

土猴子

我在山上遠望
山下那間著火的房子
房子裡住著父母兩口子
我隔著窗望
他倆在大火中有說有笑

一頭猴子從身旁的泥土裡鑽出
慌忙地亂抓遊客遺下的爛花生
牠發現了我　便怒瞪著眼
張牙舞爪地向我撲過來
我還來不及說
我還來不及說⋯⋯
　　　我還來不及說
　　　我是白樺樹啊！

　　　我還來不及說
香港猴王孫彼彼是我的⋯⋯
　　　童年玩伴

　　　我還來不及說
　　　牠也來不及看
我們臉上的疤痕

　　　我還來不及說
　　　我回來了

MONKEY OF THE SOIL

I was watching from the summit
Below was a burning room
My parents were in the room
I was watching through the window
They were chatting in the flames

From the soil nearby a monkey tunneled up
Skittishly snatching peanuts left by tourists
He discovered me and widened his eyes
Bared his teeth, prepared to pounce
Too late for me to say
Too late for me to say…

Too late to say
The white birch is me!

Too late for me to say
Hong Kong's monkey king Sun Pei Pei
Was my childhood playmate

Too late for me to say
And too late for him to see
The scars on our faces

Too late to say
I have returned

飛樹

每層樓有三十五個鳥籠，每座大樓有四十層樓，每處有五百座大樓，城裡有好多處，總共有好多好多鳥籠。夜了籠裡便逐一點燈。一盞、兩盞、三盞。隔岸望去，一城的鳥籠金光璀璨。窗外時有飛樹經過，看籠裡的孩子。鳥籠太小，我早便長出太多肉，動不了。終於有天，我打開籠伸出雙手，飛樹便接走了我。今夜，我踏著飛樹回到故籠，發現附近的小鳥都變了一頭頭大笨象，一出鳥籠便趕忙塞進升降機裡。

FLYING TREE

Every story has thirty-five birdcages, every tenement has forty stories, every place has five hundred tenements, and the city has many places, so altogether it has many, many birdcages. In the evenings, the cages are lit: one bowl of light, another bowl, a third bowl. The golden caged lights of the city are resplendent when seen from the shore. From time to time, flying trees stop by the windows to see the children within. The cages are very small; when I was little I became so big that I could no longer move inside. Then one day I opened the cage, opened my hands, and was picked up by a flying tree. Tonight, I rode back to my old cage on a flying tree, to discover that all the small birds here have grown into bumble-elephants. They jostle out of their cages, then cram into elevators.

小田雞回家

魚蛋麵裡的歡樂天地，有魚蛋，有麵條。他們在清湯裡暢泳時，赫然發現了我，便拿我開玩笑，並問我為何獨自一人。我不是一個人啊。他們說我口中有一個人的味道，臭臭的。我便轉過身來，叫身旁那個食客兼巴士司機抹掉兩條八字白鬚，他便一下子醒過來，問：「你不就是我們的小田雞嗎？小田雞你回來了嗎？」我低頭一口咬下魚蛋，說：「我就是小田雞。」

TOADIE GOING HOME

In the Wonderful World of Fishball Noodles are fishballs and noodles. They swim freely in clear soup, until suddenly they gape up at me in shock. They jockey about, ask me why I'm alone. Oh, I'm not alone. They say my mouth has the flavor of alone, a little stinky. I turn around and ask the bus driver dining beside me to erase his whitened pencil-mustache. Afterward, he awakens and says: "Aren't you our Toadie? Toadie have you returned?" I bow my head, chewing on a fishball, and say, "I am indeed Toadie."

猴
王
彼
彼

-

WAWA

-

PEI

PEI

THE

MONKEY

KING

-

32

· II

大石回來了

我背著幾個菠蘿包，爬上一座四百米的山
丘，探望一個在一千年前背著孩子走上這
山的女人。我在她身旁坐下，雙雙地唱：

山上的女人啊
放下孩子回家去吧
他在碧海裡
跟大魚追逐啊

山上的女人啊
孩子餓了回家去吧
我有麵包
你給孩子吃吧

山上的女人啊
放過孩子回家去吧
吐露港已變了陸地
漁船已在地上奔跑

山上的女人啊
我從世界的盡頭回來
告訴你他仍在海上
我聽過他的歌聲呢

女人啊　回家吧
他說外面大海很美
陽光很好
他不會回香港了

大石啊
你已等了一千年
孩子餓了
你也餓了
我們回家去吧！

THE GREAT ROCK
HAS RETURNED

Carrying pineapple buns on my back, I climbed
four hundred meters up the mountain, visiting
a woman who had carried a child up on her
back a thousand years before. I sat at her side,
singing in pairs:

Woman of the mountain *ah*
Lay down your child let's go home *ba*
He's in an emerald sea
Chasing great fish *ah*

Woman of the mountain *ah*
Baby's hungry let's go home *ba*
I have some bread
Give it to your child *ba*

Woman of the mountain *ah*
Spare the child let's go home *ba*
Tolo Harbour's all dry land now
Fishing boats race on the ground

Woman of the mountain *ah*
I've returned from world's end
To tell you he's still out at sea
I've heard his singing *ne*

Woman *ah*   Let's go home *ba*
He says the sea out there is pretty
The sunshine is fair
He won't return to Hong Kong *luh*

Great rock *ah*
You've waited one thousand years
Your child's hungry
You're also hungry
Let's return home *ba*!

白霧的弱點

唐該　請問如何通往大霧處？
哦　大霧深處沒有晴天黑夜
　　　　　沒有高低左右
你往看不見的地方走便行

唐該　請問如何在霧海游泳？
哦　霧海所及的皆沒有不同
　　　　　沒有潮漲潮退
你放心失方向失重心便行

　　　哎　驕傲的霧海啊
　　　只要樹是站著的
　　　只要我口是張開的
　　　你便會穿透我們
　　　將大樹變成神仙
　　　把我化作一陣清風
　　在白色的海田裡一起遇溺
　　雙雙沉到你的海底去

那為何你放過山下人間呢？
聽說城裡的窗總是關緊的
　　　怕你從窗口湧入
　　害他們看得太清楚！

A WEAKNESS IN THE FOG

Hi 'scuse me, may I ask how one might reach the fog?
Ah, a fog's recess has no clear day nor dark night
Has neither heights nor lefts nor rights
Just turn to the unseeable place that's the way

Hi 'scuse me, may I ask how to swim in seas of fog?
Ah, where a sea of fog reaches all difference is cleared
There's neither tide nor tide's rising
No worries abandon your center abandon direction
    that's the way

O arrogant sea of fog
So long as trees are standing
So long as my mouth is open
You permeate us
A big tree becomes an Immortal
And I a blast of cool breeze
We drown in a white seafield
Sink to your seafloor

Why then have you spared the mortal coil below
    the mount?
It's said the city's windows are all shut tight
They're afraid you'll break through
Blinding them with clear sight!

懂事的貓

仰頭見林中露出點點白光
我以為學生又用白巾上吊！

原來是從鮮草間探出的貓頭
　　　一個懂學生的貓頭
說，學生說：「我不是物件！」
　　　「我不是物件啊！」

原來是從野花間探出的貓頭
　　　一個懂工人的貓頭
說，工人說：「我不是物件！」
　　　「我不是物件啊！」

原來是從竹林間探出的貓頭
　　　一個懂司機的貓頭
說，司機說：「我不是物件！」
　　　「我不是物件啊！」

我問貓頭那他們是甚麼呢？
貓頭說他們是小樹和大樹
他們會說話　會被看不起
　　　還會造空氣！

DISCERNING CAT

Looking up I saw white gossamers poking through
    the woods
I thought a student had hanged himself with white
    cloth again!

Turns out it's a cat head poking out of fresh grass
A cat head that understands students
Saying, the students say: *I'm not an object!*
Hey, I'm no object!

Turns out it's a cat head poking out of wildflowers
A cat head that understands workers
Saying, the workers say: *I'm not an object!*
Hey, I'm no object!

Turns out it's a cat head poking out of a bamboo grove
A cat head that understands taxi drivers
Saying, the taxi drivers say: *I'm not an object!*
Hey, I'm no object!

I ask the cat head what are they then?
The cat head says they're saplings and trees
They will speak   Will be despised
And will still produce air!

毛蟲出城記

山上沒有煙火，沒有鬧劇
一條毛蟲直跳到我懷裡去

　　毛毛蟲　毛毛蟲
　　我的毛髮癢癢的
　　你要走到哪裡去？

毛蟲在我衣袖探頭四顧
走過山下鬧市、人群、商場

　　毛毛蟲　毛毛蟲
　　別讓他們看見你
　　快快躲到毛髮裡

我帶了毛蟲上船
讓荒島上的人看

　　毛毛蟲　毛毛蟲
　　我帶你看小女孩
　　留下來變蝴蝶吧！

我獨自登上回程的船
怎料毛蟲從衣領爬出

毛毛蟲　毛毛蟲
為何你不陪小女孩長大？
難道你要做大海的蝴蝶？

　　我們越過灰色的海洋
　　滂沱大雨的天空
　　終於回家洗澡去
　　肚子總覺怪怪的

　　毛蟲不見了！
她從我的肚臍鑽進去了！

CATERPILLAR
GOES TO TOWN

No fumes on the mountain, no farce
A caterpillar leaps into my arms

Catercatpill   Catercatpillar
My human hair is ticklish
Where are you trying to go?

The caterpillar pokes out from my sleeves to
      look around
Down the mountain downtown crowds and malls

Catercatpill   Catercatpillar
Don't let them see you
Quick quick hide in my hair

I take the caterpillar on a ferry
Let the barren island's people see

Catercatpill   Catercatpillar
I'll take you to a little girl
Stay behind and metamorphose!

I board the ferry back alone
The caterpillar curls out from my collar

Catercatpill   Catercatpillar
Why won't you grow up with the little girl?
Could it be you'll be a butterfly of the sea?

We surmount a gray sea
A torrential sky
To shower at home at long last
My stomach feels weird

The caterpillar's nowhere to be seen!
She drilled through my belly button!

城河飄流記

我城有一條城門河，平靜的河面上飄著
垃圾、落葉、汽車和天空的倒影。油污
在深灰色的水面蕩漾。河上方有一個
灰濛濛的太陽，一片慘白的天空，還有
幾條跟查理斯橋差很遠的泥膠橋。不
知多少戀人曾在沿河兩岸相擁接吻。

我站了一會　頭髮便多了塵埃
這河下雨時會好一點

這裡有跳橋死去的人
和一個帶帽的少年
他總是倚在河邊
望向河與天空交接的盡頭
掛著微笑哼著歌：

這河下雨時會好一點
會刮海風

這河下雨時會好一點
一顆顆垃圾會朝大海飄去

這河下雨時會好一點
一圈圈漣漪會變點點燭光

這河下雨時會好一點
垃圾會引渡孤魂到世界盡頭

下滂沱大雨最好
白鷺便能認路回家

STRANGE AND SURPRISING ADVENTURES OF THE MOAT

My city has a "City Gate Moat," or Shing Mun River. Floating on its tranquil surface are refuse, fallen leaves, the reflections of car and sky. Oil ripples on the dark gray surface. Above the river are a drizzly dust of sun, a deathly pale sky, and a few mud-glued bridges which are not remotely comparable to the Charles Bridge. Who knows how many lovers have embraced along the river's two banks—

I stand awhile while my hair collects dust
In a rain's time the river shall be fine

The suicides who've jumped are here
And a juvenile in a hat
Who always leans over the river
Longing at that end where sky and river meet
Holding a smile, humming this song:

In a rain's time the river shall be fine
And the sea wind shall stir

In a rain's time the river shall be fine
The refuse lumps shall drift out to sea

In a rain's time the river shall be fine
The ripples' rings shall become candlelight's dots

In a rain's time the river shall be fine
The refuse shall deliver these wandering souls
    to world's end

The best would be a pouring storm
For the egret knows the way home

綠氣球之死

綠色氣球在公路上唱歌
緩緩的 左一跳 右一跳
左一跳 右一跳 緩緩的
從左線移到右線
從右線飄回左線
終於由一輛的士高速輾爆

氣球的死震撼全世界
聰明的人發明了鐵傘
自此
人類又能安心細賞地上的黃花
路邊的野草、死雀、狡猾的狐狸
任何從高空墮下的人
七十五磅的吳樂兒
一百七十磅的馮寶文
五歲的李家瑩
六歲的張海俊
廿七歲的羅展鵬
五十九歲的何世
八十一歲的關正 等等
鐵傘都能把他們擋去
撐起鐵傘
便不怕從天空墮下的人
壓在自己身上
可以再次放心低頭生活
街上回復朝氣

猴王彼彼

-

WAWA

-

PEI

PEI

THE

MONKEY

KING

-

44

THE DEATH OF
GREEN BALLOON

Green Balloon singing on the highway
Gently gently   hop to the left   hop to the right
Hop to the left   hop to the right   gently gently
Inching from the left lane
Drifting from the right lane
Until a high-speed taxi pops it

The death of the balloon shook the world
Someone clever invented a steel umbrella
Henceforth
Folks could stare at yellow flowers again
Weeds in the road, dead sparrows, a sly fox
And whatever humans fall from above
Seventy-five-pound Ng Lok Yee[1]
Hundred-seventy-pound Fung Bo Man[2]
Five-year-old Lee Ka Ying[3]
Six-year-old Cheung Hoi Chun[4]
Twenty-seven-year-old Law Chin Pan[5]
Fifty-nine-year-old Ho She[6]
Eighty-one-year-old Kwan Zheng[7]   Etc.
The steel umbrella protects against them all
Raise the steel umbrella
Then we won't fear people who fall from the sky
Squashing us
We can resume a life with heads lowered
The streets back to business

---

[1] Joyful-child Ng
[2] Treasured-arts Fung
[3] Family-gleam Lee
[4] Gifted-sea Cheung
[5] Flight-of-Peng Law
[6] Era Ho
[7] Propriety Kwan

旋轉老人

中環站的爺爺
在萬馬奔騰的沙塵中
原地自轉
我上前詢問歸處
他說
他不認得路離開

MERRY-GO-ROUND
OLD MAN

The grandpa of Central Station
In the dust of ten thousand gallopings
Spins in his own gyre
I ask where home is
He says
He doesn't know the way out

猴王彼彼 - WAWA - PEI PEI THE MONKEY KING -

· **III**

狠心的大白兔

兔子先生
見你笑得如此燦爛
我心中滿是難受
你說空心的蘿蔔好吃就好吃吧
你說空心的大樹好看就好看吧
我沒有意見
只是你告訴兔孩子
地球上並沒有青草
這點我介意
有見及此
我在你家門上畫窗
讓兔孩兒看青草地
以前你會看一看窗
又看一看我
現在你只望著我笑
一直笑

HARDHEARTED RABBIT

Mister Rabbit
When I see your blunt grin
My heart is filled with pain
If you say a hollow-hearted radish is tasty then
    it's tasty
If you say a hollow-hearted tree is pretty then
    it's pretty
I have no comment
But you told the leverets
That on the earth there truly is no grass
This bothers me
And seeing as such
I drew windows on your warren door
Made the leverets see grasslands
You used to take a look at the windows
Then take a look at me
Now you just watch me and laugh
Laugh and laugh

天台國

他喜歡一個人在山頂午睡
他喜歡一個人在車頂午睡
他喜歡一個人在書頂午睡
他喜歡一個人在屋頂午睡
他喜歡在所有人的頭頂午睡

我在城裡最高和最髒的天台
沿著地上幾根剪出來的指甲
終於找到他在破花園裡午睡
「喂！我回來了！」
「起來吧！」
我朝他的臉一腳踢過去

我問他孔子別來無恙
他說他看了一天空白雲
我問他孟子可還健在
他說山裡的路不太對勁
我問他城裡還有人嗎
他說連風都走失了
但他又說
我的城市快來了
我的國快建成了

KINGDOM OF THE ROOFTOP

He likes a mountaintop siesta
He likes a cartop siesta
He likes a booktop siesta
He likes a housetop siesta
He likes siestas on everybody's heads

I'm on the city's highest, dirtiest rooftop
Tracing a few fingernail clippings
Until at last I find him napping in a
    broken garden
"Hey! I have returned!"
"Wake up!"
A kick to the face

I ask him how's Confucius been
He says he saw a sky of white clouds
I ask him is Mencius still in good shape
He says the mountain roads are not quite right
I ask him does the city still have people
He says even the wind has strayed
But he also says
My city is arriving soon
My kingdom is arising soon

鳳凰木的煩惱一

鳳凰木從嘔吐物裡長出來
我便踏著嘔吐物走上去
告訴他
一個一家三口將要死去的問題
可以是一隻小狗兩隻大狗
又可以是一隻小熊兩隻大熊
鳳凰木說
「這可是兩顆藍星一顆紅星的心情」
那我問
可以多開啟幾個宇宙嗎
這樣紅星藍星便不會死去
「但若星星不知道星星的話
宇宙是不存在的」
我一轉身
鳳凰木已伸進雲霄去

猴王彼彼

-

WAWA

-

PEI PEI

THE

MONKEY

KING

-

54

A PROBLEM FOR THE ROYAL POINCIANA I

From the vomit grows the Royal P.
So I stepped on the vomit and made my way up
To tell him a problem
There's a family of three going to die
It could be two big dogs and a puppy
It could be two big bears with a cub
The Royal P. said
It's a mood, two blue stars, one red star
So I asked
Can we unravel more universes
Where red and blue stars won't die
But if the stars don't know about stars
Universes don't exist
I turned around
The Royal P. had already stretched heavenward

鳳凰木的煩惱二

於是我對著鳳凰木的屁股
再提出一個小白兔吸毒的問題
他在雲頂裡
問這世界是否仍很奇妙
我說只要走進噪音深處
自言自語
就是最寧靜的對談
所以小白兔在人群裡吸毒
即使她雙眼反白
也是遠離死亡啊！

猴王彼彼

-

WAWA

-

PEI

PEI

THE

MONKEY

KING

-

56

A PROBLEM FOR THE ROYAL POINCIANA II

At which point I faced the phoenix tree's butt
To pose the problem of a small rabbit taking drugs
By then he was in the clouds
Asking me if the world was still wondrous
I said one need only enter clamor's depths
Speaking with oneself
To have the quietest conversation
So the small rabbit who takes drugs in a crowd
Her eyes rolling back
Means she's far from death!

撒旦與花

不得了！撒旦在課室裡上課！
課室裡的花兒還未懂得開啊！

不得了！撒旦在課室裡上課！
我一闖進課室雙腳便黏住了！

不得了！撒旦在課室裡上課！
　　我把花兒逐朵抱起
　　用前臂爬出課室
　　雙腿都拉長了！

不得了！撒旦在課室裡上課！
　　我的腿越拉越長！
　　花兒開始長出惡臉！
　　我的臉卻逐漸消失！

不得了！撒旦在課室裡上課！
　　不行了！我要消失了！
　　懷裡還有很多惡臉花朵！

MR. SATAN AND THE FLOWERS

Holy shit! Mr. Satan's schooling in the school!
The schoolflowers haven't learned to open yet!

Holy shit! Mr. Satan's schooling in the school!
I've busted in but my feet are glued down!

Holy shit! Mr. Satan's schooling in the school!
One by one I scoop the flowers up
Crawl out on my arms
Both my legs are rubbering!

Holy shit! Mr. Satan's schooling in the school!
My legs stringier and stringier!
The flowers starting to bloom evil faces!
But my face slowly vanishing!

Holy shit! Mr. Satan's schooling in the school!
Bloody hell! I'm vanishing!
My arms are still full of evil-faced flowers!

管理員之歌

深宵過後
商場的管理員是最快樂的
他去釣魚去！

深宵過後
我和速遞員是最快樂的
我們到商場看海去！

於是深宵過後
管理員遇上我和速遞員
便一同在商場的大海找大魚！

這邊有數之不盡的池魚
那邊有龍精虎猛的烏頭
管理員和速遞員興奮得手舞足蹈
我也樂得哈哈大笑！

經理醒來了！
他發現了我們
又發現了維多利亞港的魚
便把海裡的魚全部毒死

管理員已回到管理處了
速遞員已回到速遞公司去
我呢 仍守在大海上
不知死活

SONG OF THE NIGHT-WATCHMAN

After midnight
Happiest is the night-watchman of the mall
Off to fishing he will go!

After midnight
Happiest are the mailman and I
To the mall to find a sea!

Hence after midnight
The watchman runs into the mailman and me
We'll all find big fish in the mall's sea!

Endless mackerels on this side
Energetic mullets on that side
Watchman and mailman dancing with joy
Even I can't stop my laughter from roaring!

The manager has awakened!
He discovers us
And discovers fish in Victoria Harbour
And poisons all the fish in the sea

The watchman's already back to the booth
The mailman's already back to the offices
And I? Still guarding the sea
Too stupid for death

撒科羅之舞

親愛的小撒科羅
那我將小老鼠交給你
你以後要好好保護他！

親愛的小撒科羅
我在學你原地轉轉轉
把可怕的叫聲轉走吧　！

親愛的小撒科羅
我在學你原地跳跳跳
把傷痛的世界跳醒吧！

親愛的小撒科羅
若你再被拐到荒野裡
你便使勁地向前跑吧
跑到善良的地方裡去！

親愛的小撒科羅
請你叫大人不要尖叫害怕
那我便放心將小老鼠交你

DANCE OF SEVERO

Severo, little dear
In that case I'll hand you the rat
You'll have to look after him now!

Severo, little dear
I'm learning how to spin-spin-spin from you
Let's spin the shrieks of terror away!

Severo, little dear
I'm learning how to hop-hop-hop from you
Let's hop the wounded world awake!

Severo, little dear
If you're kidnapped to the wild again
Use all your might to race ahead
Race onward to a kinder place!

Severo, little dear
Tell the big scaredies no need to shriek
Then it'll be fine to hand over the rat

猴王彼彼

-

WAWA

-

PEI

PEI

THE

MONKEY

KING

-

64

· **IV**

猴王彼彼哭了

猴王彼彼哭了
那天 我長大了

那背影 一定是彼彼
牠獨坐在山坡上一角
對著山下的城市咆哮
我不敢走近

波波、原子筆、珊珊
難道他們從沒再上山嗎？
他們不就在山下的深水埗
黃大仙、又一城成家立室嗎？

那背影 一定是彼彼
牠獨坐在山坡上一角
對著山下的城市哀鳴
我低著頭 在牠身後繞過

彼彼 我回來見過你了
見你雙腿不見了
坐在天梯前發呆
我便下山去

猴王彼彼哭了
那天 我長大了
變了小孩

猴王彼彼

-

WAWA

-

PEI

PEI

THE

MONKEY

KING

-

66

PEI PEI WEPT

Pei Pei the Monkey King wept
That day, I came of age

I saw from behind   It must have been him
He sat alone on the bluff of a slope
Thundering to the city under the slope
I dared not approach

Ballpoint, Shan Shan, Bo Bo,
Could it be they've never made it back up?
Aren't they just below, in Sham Shui Po,
Wong Tai Sin, Festival Walk, building their homes?

I saw from behind   It must have been him
He sat alone on the bluff of a slope
Wailing to the city under the slope
I lowered my head, made my way around

Pei Pei, I have returned to see you
I saw you with your disappeared legs
Sitting at the stairway to heaven in a daze
And I descended

Pei Pei the Monkey King wept
That day, I came of age
And became a child

東東婆婆與了哥

東東婆婆失憶了
只剩下了哥阿福

東東婆婆失憶了
了哥阿福不停叫
「革命！革命！」

東東婆婆失憶了
把猴王彼彼繡在懷裡
了哥阿福不停叫
「革命！革命！」

東東婆婆失憶了
把猴王彼彼繡在懷裡
把山怪刻在心房
了哥阿福不停叫
「革命！革命！」

東東婆婆失憶了
忘了　忘了

東東婆婆失憶了
忘了　忘了
只剩下了哥阿福

DONG DONG GRAMMA AND MYNA

Dong Dong Gramma has forgotten *luh*
All that remains, Ah Fook the myna

Dong Dong Gramma has forgotten *luh*
Ah Fook the myna keeps crowing
Revolt! Revolt!

Dong Dong Gramma has forgotten *luh*
Pei Pei the Monkey King, sewn into her lap
Ah Fook the myna keeps crowing
Revolt! Revolt!

Dong Dong Gramma has forgotten *luh*
Pei Pei the Monkey King, sewn into her lap
The mountain spooks, engraved in her heart
Ah Fook the myna keeps crowing
Revolt! Revolt!

Dong Dong Gramma has forgotten *luh*
Don't know anymore   Don't know anymore

Dong Dong Gramma has forgotten *luh*
Don't know anymore   Don't know anymore
All that remains, Ah Fook the myna

送別金色孔雀

我登船乘風離去
從中南海至珍珠港
船上都總空無一人
便用被唾棄的泥土
造一頭金色的孔雀
孔雀吐一口氣
便生出另一頭金色孔雀

十年間
我足足擁有十艘戰艦的金色孔雀
在地球上最早和最晚的島嶼之間
那片漆黑的大海上建家
每被驅逐登岸
我便放下一頭金色孔雀
揚帆離去

FAREWELL GOLDEN PEACOCK

Aboard a ferry I ride the wind away
From the South China Sea to Pearl Harbor
The deck always empty of people
Making use then of spurned earth
I create a golden peacock
The peacock releases a breath
Which births another golden peacock

Within ten years
I've no less than ten warships full of golden peacocks
And I make my home on the pitch-black sea
Between the globe's earliest island and latest island
Each time I was expelled from shore
I set down a golden peacock
Hoisted sail and left

後記：香港神仙錄

香港當然有神仙！
要不然 我回來
鳳凰木怎會向我訴苦
毛蟲怎會掉到我身上
貓兒怎會要我安撫
白霧怎會湧我而來
猴子怎會擋我去路
小草怎會迴避我
魚蛋怎會取笑我
天台的人怎會卧著等我來
池魚和烏頭怎會撲上水面
猴王彼彼怎會坐在路中心？

香港當然有神仙啦！
要不然 我離去
鳳凰木怎會伸向天空
毛蟲怎會爬到樹頂去
貓兒怎會守在家門邊
白霧怎會向世界擴散
猴子怎會讓我去路
小草怎會偷望我
魚蛋怎會愧疚了
天台的人怎會望天抽煙
池魚烏頭怎會游出大海
猴王彼彼怎會凝望著我？

猴王彼彼

-

WAWA

-

PEI PEI

THE

MONKEY

KING

-

72

AFTERWORD: RECORD OF HONG KONG IMMORTALS

Of course Hong Kong has Immortals!
Otherwise, when I return
The royal poinciana how could it vent with me
The caterpillar how could it fall upon me
The cat how could it need my consolation
The fog how could it gush out to me
The monkey how could it obstruct my route
The little grass how could it avoid me
The fishballs how could they ridicule me
The rooftopper how could he lie down in wait for me
The mackerels and mullets how could they flood to
    the surface
Pei Pei the Monkey King how could he sit in the road?

Of course Hong Kong has Immortals *la*!
Otherwise, when I leave
The phoenix tree how could it stretch heavenward
The caterpillar how could it climb the canopies
The cat how could it guard the house door
The fog how could it disperse to the world
The monkey how could it let me pass
The little grass how could it steal a peek at me
The fishballs how could their conscience feel guilt
The rooftopper how could he stare skyward and smoke
The mackerels and mullets how could they swim out
    to sea
Pei Pei the Monkey King how could he fix his gaze
    on me?

彼彼身旁的粉筆字：

龍欣道上千人過
山坡背後萬樹春
過盡千帆皆不是
重來已是煙雲散

Past Lung Yan Road a thousand have gone
Behind a bluff ten thousand trees springing
What wends through the thousand sails is naught
Begin anew, already the smoke, the clouds, dispersing
—written in chalk beside Pei Pei

ACKNOWLEDGMENTS

"Flying Tree" first appeared bilingually in *Cha: An Asian Literary Journal*. "The Great Rock Has Returned" first appeared in translation in the anthology *Quixotica: Poems East of La Mancha*. "Pei Pei Wept" first appeared in translation in *The Margins*. The anonymous chalk poem was found written along Lung Yan Road.

Gratitude is owed to Chip-Tooth Hing, Tammy Ho, Luke Ching Chin Wai, Au Hoi Lam, Nadim Abbas, Kelly Tse and friends for their faith.

The poet also publishes under the name Lo Mei Wa.

INTERVIEW WITH THE POET

Henry Wei Leung: *A couple days ago you were reading something about extraterrestrials, a theory that Earth is a prison where the universe's unwanted souls are banished, unable to reincarnate back out there. What do you think you were banished for?*

Wawa: Extremities. I feel too easily, I love and hate to extremes, I get super mad easily, super hurt, super excited, super happy easily. I already reflected on this after reading Dostoevsky's "The Dream of a Ridiculous Man" as a teenager. I'm not cool enough to have an ultra-high intellectual extraterrestrial existence—I'm too emotional even to be a sage in this world. But I'm quite proud about my curse. This could be a fun thing during an eternal imprisonment.

HWL: *That reminds me of "Forgetting Grass," whose speaker is so overexcited while the landscape remains so cool and indifferent.*

W: It's consistent between myself and the speaker in the poem, who's like a farce, who's like a clown... But if we are all dumped souls, of course even the ants, the leaves, and the trees, they're also unwanted from outside Earth for some reason.

HWL: *I've heard people say that being a foreigner in a new country is like being a child in the world—*

W: Wait, it's me saying that to you, right?

HWL: *Well, I've heard it in different ways before.*

W: Really? I thought it was my own feeling! Oh I don't care, I don't care.

HWL: *But it's interesting. On one level we're talking about banishment, which is like the adult experience of being a foreigner; and on another level there's the child's natural feeling of estrangement. Certainly this is something you've been dealing with since moving across the Pacific last year. Would you say these elements are present in your poems too?*

W: Not really. Adults are mostly annoying and boring. They fear many things, and then they're proud and conclusive, and then they raise more adults for the world. I think the important thing is that everyone has a child in him or her, a personality that exists outside time and space—and this part resonates with the poems. Heraclitus's sense of "child" is what I always relate to: "Time is a child playing pessoi. To the child belongs the kingship."[*] An immigrant life speaks to the empirical child. The poems speak to the transcendent child.

HWL: *You usually write in English, though it's your second language. This is the first time you've written poems in Chinese. What was the urgency?*

W: I would say that—pre-Umbrella life, before 2014—I was looking for the universal, the timeless and placeless. Going through a second language, English, was a vehicle for me to arrive at this, to get myself close to an objective perspective because it's not my mother tongue... But recently when I was back in Hong Kong, I dropped my sister off to the airport

---

[*] The poet would like to thank Natasha Topaltziki for her refined translation. The original text, from Diels and Kranz fragment 52, is: αἰὼν παῖς ἐστι παίζων, πεττεύων· παιδὸς ἡ βασιληίη

and then I was free for one week. I couldn't sit still on the airport shuttle and was over-excited about where to go and play. Then I decided to hop off near Lion Rock and hike. For me this is the entrance to my home... I think there's something more complicated in saying this. It kind of implies some sort of exile, because this is where symbolically I feel my entrance of Hong Kong is—am I talking too much?

HWL: *It's your interview.*

W: I'm nervous! I feel a little artificial. So it's like when you're back after being away from home and that majestic moment when you walk into your family house. I was literally scurrying all the way to the entrance of the hike from Tai Wai. I was too excited. There were about six monkeys crouching at the entrance. I was so happy to see monkeys again so I gazed at them for so long with teary eyes until they chased me and attempted to attack. After escaping, I was still dashing uphill and talking to everything on the way during my hike: trees, butterflies, the wind, bugs. I was so excited, and inside me was this scream, *I'm back I'm back I'm back,* and I knew that nobody cares. I think it's the epitome of my relationship to Hong Kong: it's how I perceive my insignificance to this place, and still my deep love for this place.

HWL: *So why Chinese?*

W: Because the poems are talking to the ants and the grass, and it's Lion Rock: of course Cantonese rules there. If I was talking to grass in Discovery

Bay, or a fancier area like Mid-Levels, Lan Kwai Fong, maybe I'd automatically use English.

HWL: *It's an interesting transition from first saying that you were pursuing—*

W: (inaudible)

HWL: *You don't have to whisper!*

W: I feel so unnatural!

HWL: *No one's listening!*

W: There is! I know! ... 唉快0的啦！

HWL: *So first you were talking about choosing the non-mother tongue as a way to be unnatural, to alienate yourself from your worldview and reach the universal. Now you're talking about post-Umbrella, the sense of a Hong Kong identity, and finding the most natural language, which is totally different.*

W: Well, I think I would differentiate the two periods as the desire to escape from context and the desire to go back to context.

HWL: *My next question, then, is why are we having this interview in English?*

W: Because you cannot speak Cantonese!

HWL: *Hey 我得啊, 講得啊! Okay, well... Let's talk about how these are "nature" poems but not really. Not Romantic, not pastoral, and yet the natural landscape is primary in them, alive. Is this because of your relationship to Lion Rock itself, or to the natural world in a universal sense?*

W: This is how I relate to the world, not only to nature. I don't really like humans. But it's not that the world minus people is why I write about nature. I love nature but I love it not as an environmentalist, I love it how a child would love everything. I like simple and naïve and kind things that speak my language, or operate in simple formulas like, "You love me so I love you," "You hit me so I hit back." I grew up talking to wallpapers, city-mall trees, suitcases. I felt sympathy for the street lamps' loneliness. In Leiden, I talked to swan chicks in canals, and in Cologne a hyacinth committed suicide when I told her I was leaving for America. When I was younger, I'd seek out the good things in the world. If there were none, I'd imagine them, create them, so that I was never alone. Then came a stage where I saw symbols, representations, metaphors that the world was imbued with. But now, there's no division between the imagined and the real, the perceived and the objective. It's just the same thing. The caterpillar that fell inside my clothes was really taking a trip through me. I didn't get inspired by that caterpillar to write the poem, I was explaining the caterpillar's accident. There's no division between poems and reality—the poems are what I live in this reality. There's a kind of dance from Björk's *Dancer in the Dark* in my world.

HWL: *Is this reflected in your relationship to Nana, our cat who talks abnormally a lot?*

W: I think that has to do with me talking abnormally a lot to her in the first place.

This is always how you get things in the world to talk back to you, isn't it? It's you who never joins our conversations.

HWL: *The conclusion of the book in some ways is* 神仙. *The afterword asserts* 神仙 *by recalling the journey but it doesn't tell us what* 神仙 *is. Is what you're saying now a suggestion that these* 神仙 *are not beings or entities external to yourself but the vision, the journey, the dance?*

W: There are a couple poems that mention 神仙, "Immortals," and the last poem is like "proof." I think it doesn't really have anything to do with 神仙. I just want to say that this is how I look at Hong Kong. That's the first thing. Second is: this is how Hong Kong *could be seen*. Transcendentally. I mean, all these petty things, petty existences, fish, shopping malls, they're all reduced to unconscious stereotypes because we're just too used to it. Now play with all these things in the city again. No adult is watching. I'm actually realizing that what I wanted to achieve in English, this time surprisingly I achieved it through Chinese itself: I looked at the world from a way I've never looked at it before. No, language comes later. The emptier I am, the more surprisingly the world unravels itself. There's a harsh maturity that defines Hong Kong, an overabundance of "smartness." I choose to go against literary fashion, I choose creation over pessimism— like Nietzsche finally getting out from under Schopenhauer's shadow... Because of this backdrop, I side with the city's "stupid" petty things, and all this energy goes to Pei Pei, the unimportant monkey on an unimportant hill. Hong Kong, in my eyes, is very lovely. Eventually, this is the whole point: Hong Kong is so adorable, it's so cute, I'm making it lovable—even though it's so sad, it's so painful, and it's killing our kids.

HWL: *How do you see yourself in relation to Hong Kong's literary scene, and what does it mean to you to dedicate these poems to Hong Kong's children?*

W: I just do my own stuff. Nothing would make me more propelled or less propelled in writing poems. Poetry-wise, there are a handful of people I'm grateful for in Hong Kong. That's my whole relationship to it. I grew up being bullied and ostracized on so many levels. But I'd rather be a truant than a gangster at school, so I'm used to running away on my own. For poetry, I only count on the effects, on whether or not it brings something never-before-experienced, not camouflaged repetition. I hate masturbatory poetry on both individual and collective levels. It's important to stay awake. Yes, it's dedicated to Hong Kong's children. But I don't think they'll read the book, for ten thousand reasons. Local mothers talk about their kids "winning at the starting line." The kids are too busy under the watch of adults. But my dedication, as a hope and a stamp of love, does exist. If committing suicide is our kids' only exit for freedom, I'm determined to keep proving the loveliness and the strangeness of our city.

HWL: *Don't you think I should ask a question to hint to the readers that we're married?*
W: Well, no.

HWL: *You were classically trained as a singer and you got your degrees in Philosophy, with Nietzsche as your concentration. How has all this informed or misinformed your poetry?*

W: Whatever enables me to see more is what counts. What matters are the actions of "through," "over," and then "above." By then I'll have hopped and landed on something else again. In today's world everything is so systematized, taxonomized, and licensed. I can speak different languages to different categories, but to wander homelessly spitting out poems seems to be my best job in this world. To me nothing is fundamental, and nothing is ultimate. The sky is as much a scientific composition as it is an artistic composition. I love knowledge as much as I love the unknown. I love what can be seen as much as what can't be seen. I love what makes sense as much as what does not. If someone puts me in a box, I'll "why" him to death. Philosophy and music nurture my dispositions to meaning, to personality, to beauty. But there's also a me that already existed before coming to Philosophy and music. I'm one totality, one soul, one synthesizing machine that distills and empowers my own sense about everything in the universe. I'm not after one ultimate truth for mankind; I only care about the distance my sense can go. I'd thought of becoming a shepherd in Mongolia. But that's a misunderstood freedom. I'd still be imprisoned in the job. Homelessly being a poet brings me closest to the ultimate freedom, a freed soul, a freed body. An affirmative renunciation. Yes, after all, I just want to be free.

HWL: *You live in Hawai'i now, an archipelago of islands where the Native population was dispossessed and nearly wiped out by a neighboring empire. What are some of the political and emotional connections you draw between Hong Kong and here?*

W: The sea.

HWL: *What's your next project?*

W: Anything. Let's go to swim first.

TINFISH

ALSO AVAILABLE FROM
TINFISH PRESS:

Kaia Sand, *A Tale of Magicians Who Puffed Up Money that Lost its Puff* , 2016

Lissa Wolsak, *Of Beings Alone: The Eigenface*, 2016

Jonathan Stalling, *Lost Wax: Translation Through the Void*, 2015

Albert Saijo, *WOODRAT FLAT*, 2015

Norman Fischer, *Escape This Crazy Life of Tears* (Japan, July 2010), 2014

Donovan Kūhiō Colleps, *Proposed Additions*, 2014

Lehua M. Taitano, *A Bell Made of Stones*, 2013

Steve Shrader, *The Arc of the Day | The Imperfectionist*, 2013

J. Vera Lee, *Diary of Use*, 2013

Jack London is Dead: Contemporary Euro-American Poetry in Hawai'i (and Some Stories), edited by Susan M. Schultz. 2012

Ya-Wen Ho, *last edited [insert time here]*, 2012

Maged Zaher, *The Revolution Happened and You Didn't Call Me*, 2012

Jai Arun Ravine, แล้ว *and then entwine*, 2011

Elizabeth Soto, *Eulogies*, 2010

Kaia Sand, *Remember to Wave*, 2010

Daniel Tiffany, *The Dandelion Clock*, 2010

Paul Naylor, *Jammed Transmission*, 2009

Lee A. Tonouchi, *Living Pidgin: Contemplations on Pidgin Culture*, 2nd edition, 2009

Lisa Linn Kanae, *Sista Tongue*, 2nd edition, 2008

Craig Santos Perez, *from unincorporated territory [hacha]*, 2008 [out of print]

Meg Withers, *A Communion of Saints,* 2008

Hazel Smith, *The Erotics of Geography*, 2007

Linh Dinh, *All Around What Empties Out*, 2003, [out of print]. Subpress/Tinfish

Caroline Sinavaiana-Gabbard, *Alchemies of Distance*. 2001, [out of print]. Subpress/Tinfish/Institute of Pacific Studies

For other TinFish Press publications, including chapbooks and *TinFish* journals 1-20, visit our website: tinfishpress.com or order from spdbooks.org.

From the mountain peak of Lion Rock, Wawa leads us on a journey through the vibrant natural landscape of Hong Kong. These poems speak to the grass and trees, to the caterpillars and rooftops, marveling at the mundane with a child-like curiosity reminiscent of Xi Xi. Yet the specter of contemporary events—most notably the Umbrella Movement of 2014 and Fishball Revolution of 2016—is never far off, as the playful is juxtaposed with the political, homecoming with exile, and memory with loss and disappearance. Henry Wei Leung's translation beautifully captures the quiet simplicity and whimsicality of Wawa's poetry, and his detailed introduction is a must-read for anyone interested in post-Umbrella Hong Kong.

--Jennifer Feeley

Essay, poetry, translation, interview: *Pei Pei* demonstrates how rich each can be when undertaken as literary exchange. Throughout these pages, each of these literary acts informs the others, resulting in a book immanently civic in its process. Here are words not meant to be overheard, but heard directly.

--Gerald Maa

The poems in *Pei Pei the Monkey King* ping with effervescence, and zip along with all the aerial alacrity of the book's titular hero. A heady mix of fishballs, noodles, poincianas, and, yes, the irreverent monkey, Wawa has woven Hong Kong into a tapestry that is as charming as it is vivid.

--Tammy Ho